VOX HUMANA

THE STORY

OF THE

STATE HOSPITAL
PIPE ORGAN

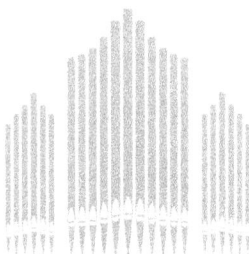

By Jason R. Carpenter

MMXXV

Arthur H. Harrington

The gifts or efforts for this undertaking are not just for today. The inspiring tones of the united voices of this instrument, or the appeal of the Vox Humana, may arouse even years hence a responsive chord in some soul, which may, for the time at least, bring relief to a disordered mind.

— Arthur Hudson Harrington, M.D.

VOX HUMANA

THE STORY

OF THE

STATE HOSPITAL
PIPE ORGAN

WITH THE COMPLETE TEXT OF

EVERLASTING LIFE

A PHANTASY

SYMBOLIZING THE MATERIAL AND
SPIRITUAL EVOLUTION
OF GENUS HOMO

BY

Dr. Arthur H. Harrington

CONTENTS

INTRODUCTION

T he afternoon sky hung low over the State Institutions at Howard, as a fine mist shrouded the grounds, blurring the outlines of red brick buildings and white clapboard cottages scattered across the landscape like a patchwork village. Yet the persistent drizzle did little to dissuade nearly two thousand guests from gathering at the grand Congregate Dining Hall, its arched windows and columned entryway rising prominently against the modest sprawl. Inside, the sound of the crowd filled the vast space, a low, steady hum reverberating beneath the towering ceilings. At the far end of the hall, the new pipe organ stood high on a balcony, drawing every eye; its polished pipes gleamed like the spires of a distant cathedral.

An unassuming plaque on the instrument bore witness to its significance: "The State Public Welfare Commission erects this plate in honor of Dr. Arthur H. Harrington, superintendent of the State Hospital for Mental Diseases, through whose untiring efforts and zeal this organ was secured. May 16, 1926."

As the last whispers faded, Mrs. Charles H. Remington of the Public Welfare Commission stepped forward to address the crowd. "When this hall was finished 25 years ago," she began, her voice clear and assured, "Dr. Harrington saw that it was incomplete without an organ. What you see here today is the vision he saw then. It is

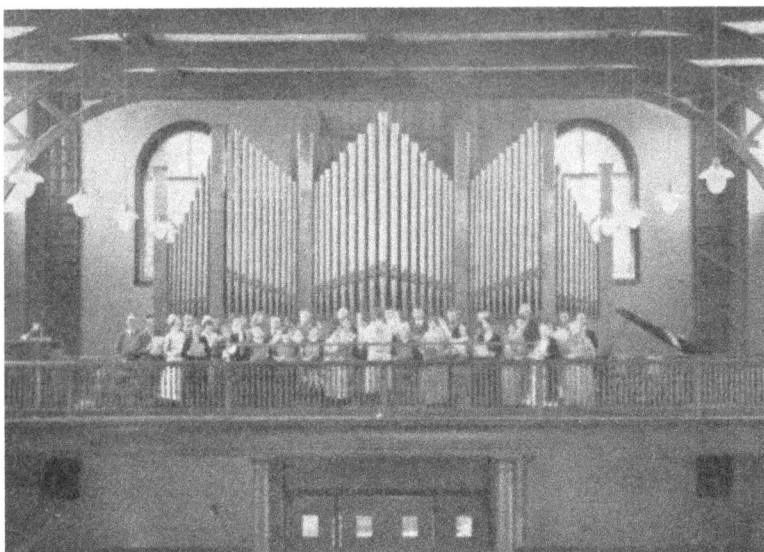

*The pipe organ on the musician's balcony of the Congregate Dining Hall,
State Hospital for Mental Diseases, 1926*

altogether through his efforts that we are able today to dedicate this organ to the service of mankind."

Thunderous applause erupted as Dr. Harrington stepped forward on the balcony, gazing out over the sea of faces below. His reputation as a pioneer in mental health preceded him, but his demeanor remained humble. "The most difficult thing about the dedication of this organ," he said, "is to put into adequate words what I feel in my heart."

"To be sure, I conceived the idea of this instrument," he continued, "but it was not I alone who put it here. It required the hearty cooperation of the Public Welfare Commission and of the general public.

"I am proud to accept the honor bestowed upon me by the Public Welfare Commission, but it is something far more than mere personal recognition. It is the recognition of a cause—the cause of music for the mentally ill."

Then, without further ado, Mr. Truesdale and Mr. Bolan, esteemed musicians both, took their places at the console. From the majestic chords of Mendelssohn's "War March of the Priests" to the delicate strains of Grieg's "Solveig's Lied," for nearly two hours, a medley of sound swept over the congregation swelling and subsiding like the rise and fall of a shared breath.

Dr. Harrington stood quietly by, his thoughts drifting back over the years—a winding path shaped by trials and triumphs, yet always guided by the vision that led him here. And as the final notes rose into the hall's vaulted heights, fading into the ether beyond the iron columns and plaster walls, the brief silence that followed seemed to hold the weight of everything that had come before; it was the culmination of a journey that began long before his tenure and would resonate long after.

Vox Humana

The state's frugality was evident from the early days of the Rhode Island State Asylum for the Incurable Insane, which opened in 1870. Established as part of a larger State Farm, the facility itself was built primarily as a cost-saving measure, intended to house the indigent mentally ill locally rather than sending them to private facilities or out-of-state institutions. By selecting a rural site, surrounded by farmland and far removed from urban centers, officials aimed to reduce expenses further, isolating patients and engaging them in simple manual labor. This approach was considered both economically beneficial and therapeutically useful.

Chronic financial struggles were a defining characteristic of the institution's history. Almost every annual report cited the shortage and underpayment of workers, poor building conditions, overcrowding, unwholesome environments, and the absence of necessary materials and equipment. Despite these persistent problems and repeated pleas for more financial support, state authorities often disregarded the Asylum's needs. By the early twentieth century, they began relying more on private philanthropy to provide basic amenities for patients, and improvements often depended on donations from the public, despite occasional appropriations.

Amid these hardships, patients endured monotonous and restrictive routines. They spent long hours seated on hard, back-to-back benches, closely monitored by attendants who patrolled the wards like sentries. Movement was limited, and during the winter months or inclement weather, this sedentary "sit-down" method was strictly enforced. On fair days, a brief walk in the yard was the extent of their physical activity.

Although other forms of therapy may have been lacking, music therapy was seemingly always a priority. Official records suggest that the program began as early as 1879, when fifty dollars were allocated for the purchase of twelve canaries and six brass cages. The birds were placed in pairs across the six halls of the institution, where they were noted to be "healthy and good singers," and where "their presence and song contributed to the happiness of the patients."

Canaries were just the beginning of the institution's engagement with music. Over the years, several pianos were donated, becoming central fixtures at patient gatherings and social activities. Eventually, the Asylum, in step with other state institutions, formed its own orchestra. Made up of both patients and attendants, the orchestra began as a five-piece ensemble but soon expanded to six instruments: piano, first violin, second violin, clarinet, cornet, and bass viol, each carefully selected to create a balanced and harmonious sound. Twice a week, this eclectic group took to the decorated stage of the assembly hall, playing against a backdrop of elaborate sets. Their performances, set amidst evenings of games and dances, became a lively occasion, offering patients a rare and welcome escape from the monotony of daily life.

Around this same period, a remarkable choir was taking shape. What began as congregational singing among several hundred patients attending chapel services soon evolved into a special group of around fifteen patients chosen for more intensive training.

The Chapel Choir of the State Hospital for the Insane, circa 1900–1912

Under the guidance of a skilled musical director, they learned melodies, practiced musical notation, and developed sight-reading skills, progressing through a curriculum like that of a high school choir. This initial, more structured approach eventually gave way to a simpler, group singing style, especially during the holidays, when familiar carols brought a sense of unity and joy that resonated deeply with the patients.

The choir, which eventually grew to about fifty voices—men and women alike—had a repertoire as varied as it was extensive, performing over two hundred selections that ranged from ballads, lyric songs, and Negro spirituals to classical pieces like Wagner's "Pilgrims' Chorus" and Sullivan's "The Lost Chord." These carefully chosen pieces avoided overly rhythmic or percussive tunes that could stir restlessness, favoring instead songs that invited emotional connection and introspection, encouraging participation while maintaining a calming influence.

By the time the choir reached its full size, their performances had become both a cornerstone of the hospital's music therapy and a cherished tradition, filling the chapel and hallways with familiar hymns and beloved melodies. Patients often found themselves humming the tunes long after the singing had ended, evidence of the music's lasting presence. It was this joyful echo of voices that soon earned the institution a new moniker: *The Singing Hospital*.

THE SHACKLES AND THE ROD

Voices lifted in mournful song from within the dimly lit assembly hall, their sound drifting into the rare stillness that had settled over the institution. Inside, more than four hundred mourners, ranging from dignitaries to former patients, gathered under the soft glow of lamplight as dusk cast long shadows across the floor. The worn wooden chairs groaned under the weight of grief-stricken bodies as all eyes were drawn to the richly adorned casket at the front. Atop it, a spray of crimson carnations rested on a bed of fern leaves, surrounded by magnificent floral arrangements that transformed the hall into a garden of sorrow. Dr. George F. Keene, the revered superintendent, lay in repose, his impact on the community evident in the solemn faces around him.

With the reverend's final blessing bringing the service to a close, the congregation rose and began to depart. After most of the people had left the hall, Dr. Keene's patients were allowed to file past their beloved physician one last time. Women came first, followed by men, many with tears in their eyes. The officers who had remained on duty also came to bid farewell, their expressions etched with grief as they gazed upon the familiar features of the man who had dedicated his life to the care of the mentally ill.

Floral Arrangements at Dr. Keene's Funeral, March 17, 1905

"*His was the task to break the shackles and the rod,*" later wrote his close friend and colleague Dr. Henry Jones, "*and lift them from the back and limbs of those poor, demented, witless children of his God.*"

Though Dr. Keene's 17-year tenure ended in relentless battle against adversity, it was also a period of profound transformation. And while his passing marked the end of an era, his legacy would endure in the very foundations of the asylum he transformed.

As the early 1900s dawned, the institution, now known as the State Hospital for the Insane, continued to confront unremitting challenges. The wards, packed to capacity, overflowed with patients in various states of distress and disarray. Tuberculosis and typhoid fever ran rampant among the vulnerable population, claiming lives without mercy. The dilapidated facilities barely functioned, and the constant threat of illness loomed over everything.

In response to these dire conditions, Dr. Keene had spearheaded the first major construction project in nearly half a century, which included a new administration and service building, a new hospital ward, and, most remarkably, a congregate dining hall. Planned in 1900 and completed in 1904, the dining hall stood out as a notable architectural feat, providing a communal space that also allowed for the conversion of smaller dining rooms in the old pavilions into much-needed sleeping quarters, marking a significant step toward easing the overcrowding that had long plagued the institution.

But the relentless cycle of sickness and death weighed heavily on Dr. Keene, and the demands of his role, along with constant exposure to the institution's harsh conditions, eventually took a toll on his health. Just six months after the dining hall's inauguration, in early March 1905, he fell gravely ill and succumbed to pneumonia. His sudden death thrust the institution into uncertainty, and the heavy burden of leadership soon fell to his assistant, Dr. Fred Jewett, whose brief tenure would end in scandal.

Among the patients at this time was William Morse, a former prison guard who had been committed to the hospital after being found legally unaccountable for the murder of Julia Toombs. Once romantically involved, Morse's affection for Miss Toombs twisted into a dangerous obsession after she refused his hand in marriage. After months of harassment, their relationship reached a breaking point. In broad daylight, as she made her way to church, Morse approached her on a busy street in Providence and, before horrified onlookers, shot her three times in the back with a revolver, ending her life in a shocking act of madness.

Pursued and captured by stunned witnesses, Morse was taken to prison and indicted for murder. However, the court deemed him too unstable for conventional justice, and he was remanded to the State

Hospital, where his volatile behavior would soon test the limits of Jewett's methods.

As a free man, Morse was known for his rational demeanor, keeping his temper tolerably well, though in recent months he had grown increasingly melancholy over the failed love affair. This facade of self-control, however, unraveled during his legal proceedings. Described as "a giant in size," it took six strong men to restrain his violent, curse-laden outbursts at the arraignment, during which he made no secret of his loathing for the State Hospital, vowing that if ever committed there, he would kill the superintendent. Once institutionalized, his resentment only grew. As a patient, his anger simmered, often bubbling to the surface in explosive, exhausting outbursts. During one such episode, he directed a string of insults at an attendant, who promptly reported the incident to Jewett. In response, Jewett ordered Morse strapped into a straitjacket and confined to a cell, in which he remained for eight consecutive days, wracked in suffocating confinement.

When the State Board of Charities and Corrections learned of this prolonged restraint, they launched an investigation. During the hearing, Jewett admitted that he had instructed Morse to be "tied up" until he apologized. The Board unanimously moved to dismiss the superintendent, condemning the excessive punishment, stating it was "unreasonable to expect an apology from an insane person."

Such abuses were notoriously common in the institutional care of the mentally ill during that period, and the severe conditions and widespread mistreatment frequently reported at the State Hospital underscored the necessity for significant change. Recognizing this urgent need, state authorities sought a leader capable of driving true reform.

The man chosen for this formidable task, Dr. Arthur H. Harrington, brought a fresh perspective and a wealth of expertise to the institution. A Brown University graduate and accomplished physician, Harrington had extensive experience from his work at Danvers State Hospital, where "he laid the broad and deep foundations of his knowledge of psychology and psychiatry" as Superintendent. At the Bridgewater State Farm, his tenure was similarly distinguished by "converting it from a purely custodial penal institution into a true hospital," organizing the separation of criminally insane patients transferred from the State Lunatic Asylum at Worcester from the non-criminal paupers.

These experiences proved instrumental when he assumed his role at Howard. As superintendent, Harrington initiated significant reforms to improve patient care. He expanded the medical staff, established a training school for nurses, and advocated for a parole system, allowing patients to leave the hospital for up to six months. He also encouraged family placements, where individuals were paid to board patients in their homes. In line with key goals of the then emerging mental hygiene movement, he advocated for the establishment of psychopathic hospitals in urban areas and brought social workers into the institution, assigning them to patient discharge planning and the collection of patient histories, reflecting his belief that heredity played a significant role in mental illness. Perhaps most tellingly, at Harrington's suggestion, the institution was renamed in 1912 from the State Hospital for the Insane to the State Hospital for Mental Diseases.

Harrington's ambitions, however, often exceeded the state's budget. Many of his recommendations, including the construction of a separate building for tubercular patients, were not realized due to financial constraints. The state's unwillingness to increase staff pay, despite his urging, also hindered efforts to attract and retain quality attendants. Undeterred by these limitations, he nevertheless remained committed to improving patient care, advocating that strategic investments could lead to long-term cost savings by facilitating discharges and reducing the need for prolonged hospitalization.

MUSIC AS RATIONAL THERAPY

As mental health practices evolved in the early 20th century, forward-thinking practitioners sought new approaches to treatment. Dr. Harrington, though aware that music therapy had a long history across many cultures, recognized that its potential remained largely untapped in contemporary practice. Even so, as a musician himself, he believed passionately in its potential. His conviction was simple yet compelling: music, instinctive across all cultures and times, must hold the key to reaching what he termed "disordered minds."

Drawing a parallel between music and medicinal substances, he observed that drugs remain inert until "brought into contact with the tissues of the body," whereupon they "emerge as forces." Music, he believed, could function similarly. When administered under careful control and wise direction, music was the transmutation of material substance into a force, capable of releasing energies that manifest in various parts of the body, evoking a range of emotional and physical responses. "It matters not whether it comes from a singing rock, a musical valley, a singing teakettle, a Stradivarius violin, or the human larynx," he said. Music's effects on the human organism were corporeal, and held valuable therapeutic properties justifying its use as a rational therapy for the mentally ill.

Among the various forms of musical expression, Dr. Harrington held a special place for singing, valuing it particularly for its curative potential. He noted that singing stimulated respiration and heart action, which increased oxygenation to the tissues producing a benign effect upon morbid mental states. Promoting deep breathing and relaxation, singing, he claimed, was particularly beneficial for patients suffering from anxiety, helping them approach other tasks with renewed interest, while the disciplinary effect of the necessary drilling helped them regain self-control.

Dr. Harrington saw singing as especially powerful in fostering a sense of community among patients. He believed that group singing sessions offered a collective form of expression that helped to break down feelings of isolation often associated with mental illness. This communal aspect of singing, he asserted, enhanced social interaction and reinforced the therapeutic benefits of music by creating a supportive environment where patients could share their voices and experiences. Moreover, singing required no special equipment, making it an accessible form of therapy that could be easily integrated into daily routines.

Thus, under his guidance, concerts by the hospital choir on Sunday evenings after supper became a beloved ritual, recalling the choir's early days in the chapel, with many patients spontaneously joining in to create a harmonious and spirited sound. As such gatherings grew in popularity and significance, the Congregate Dining Hall became the central venue for this and other musical experiments.

A Magnificent Instrument

The Congregate Dining Hall was a marvel of both design and functionality. Unlike the hospital's 40-year-old, one-story wooden pavilions that were cold, dark, and unsanitary, the hall was spacious, with large transom windows for ample natural light and ventilation. The walls were painted in terracotta, and the ceilings in beige tones to enhance the sense of space, creating a pleasant and healthful

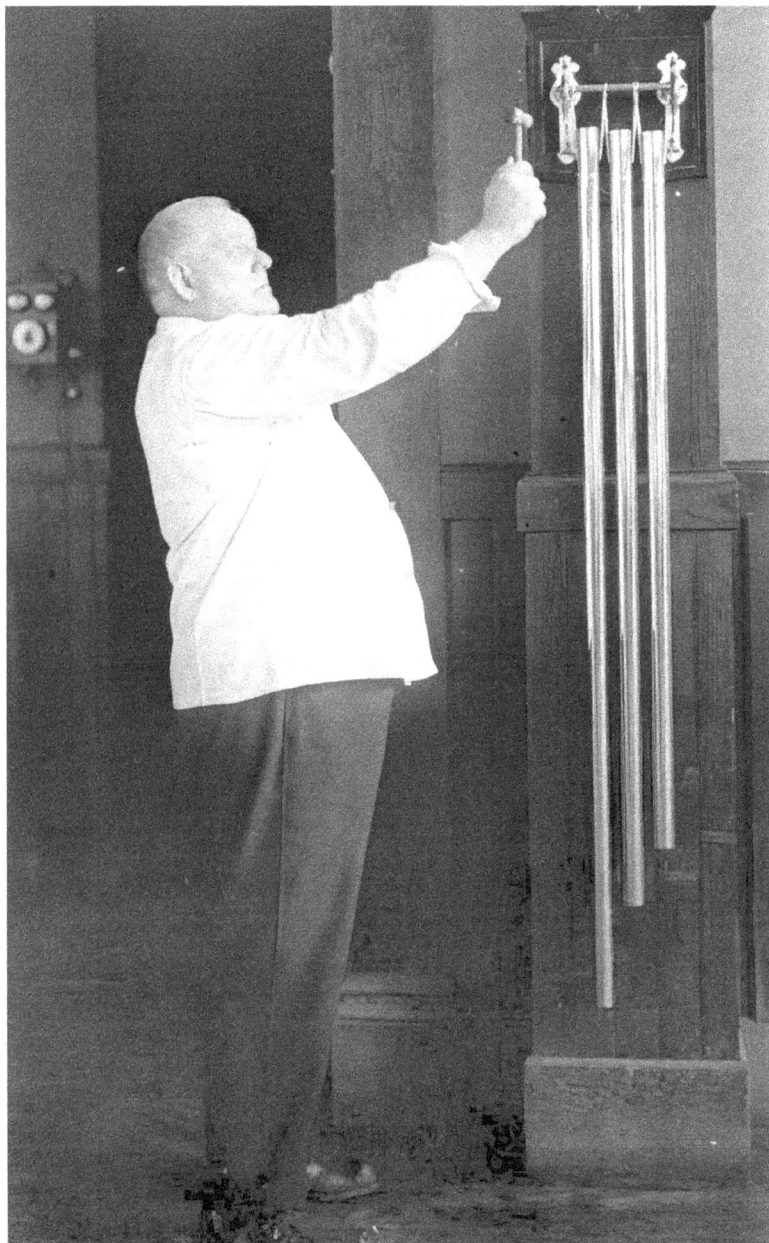

The playing of tubular chimes is the signal for each of the several steps in the serving of a meal in the Congregate Dining Hall.

The Congregate Dining Hall at the State Hospital for Mental Diseases circa 1900–1912, before the installation of the pipe organ

atmosphere. The hall's dimensions were impressive, with a floor space of 146 by 100 feet and a vaulted ceiling reaching 39 feet at its center, supported by seven iron columns on each side, adorned with decorative brackets. Circular shelves around the columns held potted flowers and ferns, adding to the aesthetic appeal.

This expansive facility, capable of accommodating over a thousand people, functioned as both a dining area and a space for entertainment, in which music was seamlessly integrated into the environment. On one side of the hall stood a stage, large enough for a small orchestra and suggestive of a playhouse theater, equipped with curtains, flies, and a painted backdrop. On the opposite end, there was a balcony where visitors could observe the activities below. Beneath the vaulted ceiling, public concerts graced the stage on special occasions, while the hospital orchestra's daily performances created an orderly and uplifting atmosphere during mealtimes.

Beyond its aesthetic appeal, the hall's design also prioritized practicality and comfort. Heating was efficiently managed by radiators housed in iron boxes beneath slate shelves that ran the length of the hall. During mealtimes, food brought in on carts was placed on the warm shelves before distribution, ensuring the crockery was heated. Fifty-six tables, each seating sixteen people, were arranged in orderly rows. The layout split the hall into two main sections, with a broad aisle running down the center, separating the men on one side from the women on the other. When patients entered the dining hall, the only articles at each place setting were a cup, saucer, and drinking glass.

The mid-day meal for patients, lasting precisely one hour, was a model of efficiency and order. As visitors entered the gallery above the serving room, they could see the flow of activity spilling from the corridor connecting to the main kitchen and bakery, a seamless coordination of movements that kept everything running smoothly. Likewise, each stage of the meal followed a carefully timed choreography, orchestrated by slender tubular chimes that rang in harmonious intervals—the first, third, and fifth notes of the scale.

At 11:25 a.m., the first signal chimed, marking the beginning of the meal, and patients, segregated by sex, entered through four different doors to the sound of marching music played by the orchestra. After all the patients were quietly seated, a second signal rang out, indicating that nurses were distributing silverware. The third signal marked the start of food service, with subsequent chimes indicating the progression of different courses.

The music that accompanied the meal began with lively and spirited compositions during its initial stages. As service progressed, the melodies shifted to more subdued pieces without marked time. This careful selection and order of music ensured a gradual progression towards pianissimo, descending to a quiet conclusion. At 12:20, the tubular chimes signaled that it was time for the patients to depart. The orchestra switched to marches again as each table was dismissed by a supervisor, and the patients left in the same manner they had entered.

As Dr. Harrington sat in the corner of the dining hall, he watched both patients and attendants move with the precision of a well-tuned machine. Strings and brass filled the hall with their harmonies, punctuated by the rhythmic clink of cutlery against plates. The nurses, like conductors in an intricate symphony, directed the flow of dishes with a practiced ease that belied the sheer number of mouths to feed, their movements a graceful dance of refined coordination.

Stirred by this daily ballet set to melody, a vision began to form in his mind: a new musical centerpiece for the institution—a magnificent instrument capable of amplifying this almost mystical power he so faithfully witnessed.

Little did he know, the realization of this vision would mark the beginning, and the end, of another defining chapter in the institution's history.

THE STORY OF THE STATE HOSPITAL PIPE ORGAN

In 1920, Dr. Harrington stood before the Penal and Charitable Commission with a bold proposal: to acquire a suitable pipe organ for the State Hospital for Mental Diseases—not through state funds, but entirely through voluntary donations.

To his surprise, the commission, well aware of the state's limited resources and reluctance to fund non-essential projects, wholeheartedly endorsed the plan. Recognizing the necessity of relying on external contributions, they not only backed the proposal but also granted him full authority to conduct fundraising and planning activities. Emboldened by this unexpected support, he set an ambitious budget of $10,000, deemed necessary to purchase an instrument that would serve as both a therapeutic tool and an architectural centerpiece, enhancing the dining hall's design while fulfilling its vital musical function.

With the budget set and the task of executing the plan ahead, Harrington knew that achieving this goal would require financial contributions and active support from both patients and the public alike. Ever resourceful, he began to explore every corner of the hospital grounds for overlooked assets, thus setting the stage for a series of creative fundraising efforts that would galvanize the community and bring his vision to life.

Sweet Orchard Honey

At the far reaches of the institution's expansive property, nestled among the overgrowth and wildflowers, stood a few weathered beehives—remnants of a farm purchased by the state years earlier. Long neglected, they had only sporadically yielded honey, and the Hospital's farmer, lacking apiculture skills, managed little more than a few pounds each season.

Upon discovering the forgotten apiary, Dr. Harrington saw in it a chance to support the pipe organ fund in an unexpected way. Determined to turn it into something of value, he enlisted the help of Mrs. Florence Hinckley, a seasoned beekeeper from the State Agricultural College, trusting her expertise to restore the colony to productivity.

The restoration work began promptly, and, under Mrs. Hinckley's skilled care, the beekeeping operation soon flourished. Honey production increased, and the first year's modest profits—half of which became the very first contribution to the fund—marked a promising start.

"For thousands of years," Dr. Harrington mused, "bees have gathered sweets from the blooms of the fields; time and circumstances have made their descendants our contributors."

True to this ancient tradition, the bees' quiet labor continued year after year, adding to the fund with each season's jars of golden nectar, labeled "Sweet Orchard Honey from State Hospital Apiaries, Howard, Rhode Island."

Encouraged by this small success, Dr. Harrington began to wonder what other hidden treasures might lie undiscovered within the institution's vast and storied grounds. With renewed curiosity, he turned his focus to other overlooked corners. His search soon led him to the attic.

A LOOM IN THE ATTIC

In the quiet of the hospital's attic, time seemed to stand still, preserving memories of a bygone era when lanterns cast their warm glow on spinning wheels, and grandmothers wove homespun fabric on sturdy looms. It was there in the gloom, draped in cobwebs and shadows, that Dr. Harrington's eyes lit up with excitement as he discovered just such a loom hidden in a dusty corner. At once, he called for assistance, and together with a patient experienced as a mill-weaver, they brought it out, assembled it, and set it up for use once again.

As time passed, the old loom became the centerpiece of a growing initiative that expanded well beyond its humble beginnings. What started with a single, dust-covered relic soon multiplied. Additional looms joined the first—their number eventually reaching ten—while workshops for other crafts took root alongside them. Spreading across four large rooms, the program grew to include skilled instructors guiding more than 300 patients in creating a wide variety of items. From practical goods made from salvaged materials to intricate pieces that captivated onlookers at agricultural fairs, their output was as diverse as it was impressive.

In observing the program's success, Dr. Harrington noted its impact on patients' well-being. Engaging in meaningful work grounded them in reality, he claimed, shifting their focus away from what he called "morbid ideas and delusions." The transformation was particularly striking in those from the most disturbed wards. Once destructive and requiring constant supervision, many of these patients now not only cared for themselves but also found purpose working in special hospital departments.

This work, which became known as "occupational therapy," yielded remarkable results. In just a few short years, the patients' industriousness had produced more than 44,000 items. Many of these were used within the Hospital, while others—beautiful examples of fancy-work, toys, baskets, and rugs—were sold at local markets. By 1925, the surplus from their sale, combined with proceeds from the hospital's beekeeping, amounted to $2,000, marking a significant milestone: one-fifth of the fund's goal had been raised through these efforts alone, even before a single donation had been sought.

Further inspired by this achievement, Dr. Harrington conceived his next visionary plan—a daring venture that would carry their message even further beyond the Hospital's grounds.

Voices Ready to Make History

On the evening of October 9, 1925, the recording studio at WJAR, The Outlet Company, buzzed with anticipation. Forty-four patients from the State Hospital for Mental Diseases, dressed in their best attire, filled the room. Led by Mrs. Karl Sturgis, the Hospital's music director, and accompanied by the blind pianist Harry Kenyon, the choir stood ready to make history.

As final preparations were made, the patients murmured among themselves, their words barely rising above a nervous whisper, while technicians moved with practiced efficiency, ensuring every microphone was in place, every cable connected, and every dial set to perfection. Warm studio lights reflected off their eager faces.

The patients had arrived by trolley, traveling fourteen miles from the Hospital to the heart of downtown Providence. For many, it was their first time beyond the institution's walls in years. After months of rigorous training, they were prepared at last to share their progress with an unseen audience, reaching distant places they could only imagine.

Mrs. Sturgis, calm amidst the flurry of activity, gave final instructions to the choir, her steady confidence uprighting the group. Nearby, Mr. Kenyon settled at the piano, fingers poised at the keys, his unseeing eyes focused inward on the music to come.

As the final seconds ticked away, the studio fell silent. The patients took their places, and the red On Air light flickered on. Mrs. Sturgis raised her hands, and a collective breath was held.

Breaking Free Through Music

For over thirty minutes, the patients' voices filled the airwaves with nine carefully selected musical numbers. From the joyous refrains of Thank God for a Garden to the bittersweet resolve of Smiling Through, their performance was an astonishing display of talent and dedication. John Archer, an accomplished composer and respected figure in the local music community, later remarked, "It was one of the most inspiring things I had ever witnessed."

As the broadcast drew to a close, Dr. Harrington stepped forward to address the listeners, his voice steady with conviction. "I think we have shown this evening," he started, "what is possible to do in a hospital of this kind through the use of music, particularly in a vocal way." He then spoke of the effort to fund a new organ, expressing hope that the evening's performance would inspire their contribution.

Turning to the choir, Dr. Harrington asked if they had any message for the radio audience. One voice from the back of the group enthusiastically replied, "Tell them we are glad to get down street and we hope they enjoyed our singing," to which they all gave a prompt and hearty assent.

The patients' return to the hospital that night was uneventful. Back at the Congregate Dining Hall, as they sat down to enjoy a well-earned celebratory feast, a sense of profound accomplishment fell over them.

For this brief time, they were not confined by their diagnoses or circumstances. They had become singers and performers, capable of moving hearts and minds with their voices.

UNEXPECTED NEWS

In the days and weeks that followed, donations large and small poured in from every corner of the state, coming from donation boxes, local businesses, churches, and charities. But while the early wave of support was encouraging, as autumn turned to winter, the initial surge of support began to wane.

Undeterred, Dr. Harrington returned to the studio to renew his appeals, taking solace in the steady stream of modest donations that continued to arrive. He had even heard that the broadcast had reached beyond the Canadian border, fueling his belief in the campaign's ultimate success, even as the fundraising efforts stretched on. "The goal, though still seemingly far away," he said, "was luminous with hope."

It was during this period, as concerns began to grow about the campaign's progress, that a telephone message brought unexpected news. An acquaintance informed Dr. Harrington about a modern organ that might be available for purchase and asked if it would interest him. Intrigued, he wasted no time in arranging to inspect the instrument, cautiously optimistic that it could meet his needs.

At the Imperial Theatre in Pawtucket, Dr. Harrington found the organ to be a remarkable instrument, exceptional in its quality and potential. However, not wanting to make a hasty decision, he sought the expert opinions of two prominent musicians and organists. Their assessments only confirmed his initial impressions. "It's an honest piece of work," one wrote, "the stops are all real speaking ones, and they build to a satisfactory ensemble." The other praised its "ample power and variety of voicing," remarking that they doubted "if you could find anything equaling it at the price in our broad land."

The organ was indeed an exquisite specimen of craftsmanship and technology. Originally built around 1915 by the Hall Organ Company of West Haven, Connecticut, as a gift to St. John's Church in Great Barrington, Massachusetts, the organ was later rebuilt by the William W. Laws Organ Company of Beverly before finding its new home at the theater in 1920. The renovation retained the fundamental parts of the instrument, including the pipes and wind chests, but introduced modern advancements, such as pneumatic action and electric actuation. With three manuals and twenty-eight speaking stops, complete with sub and super couplers, its range was further expanded by the addition of a choir organ, harp, chime, and xylophone.

In a pivotal radio address on November 5, Dr. Harrington shared the extraordinary offer presented to him by Mr. Thomas E. Marsden, a well-known Providence citizen, philanthropist, and proprietor of the theater where the organ was installed. "The owner of this organ is offered today, by some interests who desire to acquire it, practically what it cost five years ago," he explained, "but he wants the State Hospital to have it. He will, for the sum of $7,500, transport the instrument to the Hospital and set it up in the musicians' balcony in the Congregate Dining Hall, ready to play, and he will do the installing without extra compensation from any source whatever."

Remarkably, Marsden extended this generous proposal despite the Hospital's fund falling short of the asking price. His sympathetic offer included no fixed deadline for final payment, no interest charges, and the commitment that the organ would remain in place as long as both it and the building endured.

The pipe organ and choir at the Congregate Dining Hall,
State Hospital for Mental Diseases, 1926

By December, the purchase arrangements were concluded; and with the agreement in place, the transportation and installation of the organ began. At its end, the project found another ally in Mr. John Bolan, a member of the State Public Welfare Commission. An experienced organist and former church organ builder himself, Mr. Bolan volunteered his time and expertise, supervising every detail of the work and even designing the organ's case. For weeks, he spent his evenings at the Hospital, ensuring that the operation proceeded smoothly and that the organ would be ready to fill the hall with its music on its inaugural day.

Thus, on a rainy spring afternoon in May of 1926, the Congregate Dining Hall of the State Hospital was transformed at last. After five years of planning and effort, there it stood: the organ, with its five gleaming panels of gilt pipes set in an oak case of unpretentious yet artistic design, occupying the musician's balcony. With an impressive frontage of 27 feet and reaching a height of 19 feet from base to top, it commanded the hall—a towering edifice of burnished metal and polished wood.

As final preparations for the dedication concert were underway, Dr. Harrington, surveying the hall one last time, marveled at how far their message had spread in just a few months. "Time was when primitive man communicated with his fellows by a few broken syllables," he mused. "Today the human voice is carried in connected speech from one continent to another; the wonderful discovery of the radio was called to our aid and we are unaware of how far this story has traveled by that means." Pausing for a moment, he allowed himself a brief, satisfied smile.

FINALE

Recalling the sudden loss of Dr. Keene decades earlier, the Hospital once again faced uncertainty at a pivotal moment in its history. Barely two months after the organ's dedication, in July of 1926, Dr. Harrington unexpectedly resigned as superintendent of the State Hospital for Mental Diseases. Citing "personal reasons," his abrupt departure puzzled many, though rumors of his ill health quietly circulated. Friends and colleagues, eager to retain his expertise, nevertheless persuaded him to stay on as a consulting psychiatrist; yet, despite his continued association with the Hospital, his stepping down marked the end of another era.

The appointment of his successor, Dr. Ransom Sartwell, was initially met with optimism. A highly credentialed medical doctor with a distinguished career, Sartwell had previously served as Assistant Superintendent at the Worcester State Hospital and as Superintendent of the State Infirmary at Howard. His leadership was expected to continue the progressive trajectory established by Dr. Harrington. However, his administration soon became embroiled in scandal.

The controversy erupted when Sartwell made the ill-fated decision to hire a physician named Dr. Sarat Mukerji, whose qualifications were the subject of skepticism among hospital officials. While Mukerji reportedly produced a medical diploma from India, doubts lingered about its authenticity. The pathologist, whose prior experience in the United States was limited to administering drugs to guinea pigs and observing their effects in a New York hospital laboratory, was intended to be part of Sartwell's plan to establish a syphilis research lab. However, Mukerji's incompetence quickly became apparent. He misread X-ray films and failed to diagnose a clear shoulder dislocation and fracture in one patient. The injury went untreated for months until a visiting surgeon from Providence corrected it. Worse yet, he mishandled critical Wasserman tests, essential for diagnosing syphilis. Lab technicians, frustrated by delays, insisted the work be transferred to state-run facilities at the Capitol. But it was during an autopsy that Mukerji's lack of medical competency was laid bare. Struggling to begin the incision on the cadaver, he fumbled in front of two observing doctors. Appalled by the display, one of the doctors leaked the incident to the Providence Journal, igniting a media firestorm.

Though the public outcry forced Sartwell to dismiss Mukerji, the damage was done. A committee was swiftly formed to investigate the conditions at the State Hospital and other state institutions. Their report was scathing. In a familiar refrain, it revealed that the Hospital's facilities were antiquated and grossly overcrowded, with gravely ill patients, particularly those with tuberculosis, being "herded" into wards with well patients. Moreover, the report highlighted an alarmingly high death rate—levels not seen since the 1890s. Compounding the situation was the institution's inability to adequately segregate violent patients—a critical oversight that Dr. Harrington had pointed out years earlier.

"The fact is that we have no proper place in which to keep patients technically known as criminally insane," he said. "Warden Linscott of the State prison and I both recommended an appropriation of $225,000 for a custodial hospital last fall... The proposal for that issue still rests in the House finance committee, dead."

While the final details of the investigation were made public in early January 1929, Dr. Sartwell had little opportunity to respond. A week and a half later, on the evening of January 11, returning from a "Fathers' Night" meeting at a local church, he entered his residence on the hospital grounds. Seated alone in the living room, the window shades undrawn as he prepared to write a telegram, Sartwell became an easy target for an escaped patient lurking outside. Armed with a stolen double-barrel shotgun, the assailant crept outside the house, positioned himself at the window, and fired a single shot, killing the superintendent almost instantly.

The "Mad Houdini," Frank Weeden—a notorious fugitive and inventor by his own claim—had vanished more than a year prior, following his fifteenth daring escape from the institution. In his absence, rumors of his whereabouts ran rampant, with alleged sightings reported across the state. Some believed he had fled the region, while others yet whispered of his demise. It was against this backdrop of suspicion and speculation that Weeden made his calculated return to the hospital grounds, driven by a twisted desire for revenge against Sartwell, who had denied his parole. His capture at gunpoint outside the home of his aged and broken-hearted mother did little to quell the fear and outrage sparked by the slaying of a public official.

At his arraignment, Weeden exhibited a chilling indifference, even intoning a sense of pride as he openly confessed to the murder. "I'm certainly glad I did it," he told the judge, "And I feel that I've made a good start." As the proceedings continued, it was revealed that Harrington's name was one among several on his kill list; a reign of terror at the State Institutions had been narrowly averted.

Despite Weeden's confession and the evidence against him, a jury found him not guilty by reason of insanity, and once more he was committed to the State Hospital. Consigned, this time, to solitary confinement, he was imprisoned in a cubicle of masonry and iron bars in the State Prison yard, and held under close guard. But even these strict measures couldn't stop his final disappearing act. Two days before Christmas, the homicidal maniac and Mad Houdini of Howard, Rhode Island, was found hanged in his cell, his bedclothes wrapped tightly around his neck.

In the aftermath, plans were swiftly put into motion to construct a new ward specifically designed for the criminally insane. The remodeled east wing of the Women's Reformatory building was transformed into what was described as "the most modern hospital for mental diseases that could be built," and at the same time, a carefully planned prison. The ward included nineteen cells, each fortified with combination iron and wood doors weighing 387 pounds, with glass windows reinforced by a fly-mesh screen. In front of each door, a heavy-gauge latticework cage was installed, with a pick-proof lock situated between the cage and an outer glass window, accessible only to an attendant with a long key, and if a patient somehow broke through both the caging and windows, they would still be confronted by iron bars an inch thick. The cells themselves were designed with smooth, seamless walls and floors, devoid of any projections or knobs that could be used for self-harm or as a means of hanging. Even the radiators were built into the walls, rendering them inaccessible.

For the most dangerously violent patients, two special cells were constructed with walls of combined cement and plaster, designed to withstand any attempts to damage them. Even the underground tunnels, which connected the ward to the rest of the institution, were secured with iron-barred doors, no two of which were ever open at the same time. Every aspect of the ward was engineered with the memory of Weeden's escapes in mind, making any future attempt futile.

As the Hospital entered a new chapter, broader transformations began to take shape. The Great Depression—despite its hardships—

brought federal funds that enabled other long-deferred improvements to finally materialize. Though no longer superintendent, Dr. Harrington remained a guiding force in shaping the Hospital's future. Week after week, he and Sartwell's successor, Dr. Arthur P. Noyes, worked together to bring long-envisioned improvements to life. By the mid-1930s, their efforts culminated in twenty-two new buildings, each addressing critical needs recognized for years but previously impossible to meet due to lack of funding. The hospital Harrington had imagined for decades was finally taking shape.

In his waning years, Dr. Harrington found time to pursue other long-held aspirations. Unknown to even his closest friends, he had long been working on an ambitious opus that comprised four poems in heroic verse, accompanied by around twenty interpretative musical scores. Rooted in Norse mythology, the work explored the origins of life on Earth, beginning with the Ice Age and capturing the eternal cycles of growth and renewal through the rhythm of the seasons. Though the text was completed, the music would remain forever unfinished. He titled this incomplete masterpiece Everlasting Life.

On March 12, 1939, despite years of failing health, Dr. Harrington had been in good spirits throughout the day. In the evening, at his home, he gathered with friends to share his completed poems before sitting at the piano to play one of his own scores. After only a few bars, he suddenly paused. His hands fell still on the keys. Complaining of feeling ill, he rose and made his way to his room. There, he lay down upon his bed and, in two or three minutes, quietly passed away at the age of eighty-two.

"He had really died at the piano with his beloved music," it was later recalled. "No pain, no suffering, and no lingering sickness."

"Just Rest and Peace!"

EPILOGUE

"It's public property," my guide called back, already several steps ahead, confident as he crossed the green. A few hundred yards away, inmates in white t-shirts and khaki pants lingered behind a tall chain-link fence crowned with razor wire. One of them was painting a picnic table, one in a long row of tables propped on their ends. A voice came through a far-off loudspeaker, muffled and indistinct, its commands barely audible at this range.

I quickened my pace, stepping onto a narrow walkway that disappeared into a thicket where the remnants of something long gone lay hidden. An isolated gravel path stretched across the wide open field, passing by a well covered with a rusted metal plank. Here was once the site of the walled-in hospital for the insane, known as "the sheep pen."

"Sometimes, you find homeless people here." He pointed to a cluster of bushy overgrowth. The path through it was littered with plastic bottles, rags, and crushed aluminum cans. "They're friendly," he reassured me. "I just talk to them."

As the morning's cool air began to give way to the rising heat of the summer sun, we paused at the corner of Keene Avenue and Harrington Road, a nearly deserted stretch at the rear of the grounds running north between the old employee dormitories and prison yard.

Howard Avenue in Cranston, Rhode Island, 2024

Nearby, the steady hiss of steam escaped from a fenced vent where it rose from underground, the sound mingling with the rustle of leaves stirred by a breeze. Birdsong from hidden perches in the treetops contrasted with the distant hum of industry—a reminder that beyond these grounds, the rhythm of daily life goes on.

Harrington Hall was just ahead, the building quiet in a way that felt unusual. Typically, a shuffling throng could be seen lined up outside or milling about the place, but today the activity had stilled.

A short walk past the old hospital buildings brought us to a vast, empty parking lot where the congregate dining hall once stood. I stood where the pipe organ had once been, the sun beating down on the asphalt of this shadeless expanse. High above, an airplane passed by, a faint droning swallowed by the open sky.

"Over there was the stage," I said, motioning to a line of yellow snow plows parked along the lot's overgrown edge, idle and ready for winter.

It was hard to imagine what all of this had been in another life.

This was the historic farming village of Howard, in the city of Cranston, where Rhode Island's State Farm was hewn from hallowed ground. Fieldstones, hoisted by the hands of generations of paupers and prisoners, laid the foundations. Ironically, many of their remains now lie a short distance away, buried beneath rows of numbered stones that mark their anonymous and unremembered graves.

So too are forgotten the emblems of unfulfilled dreams that often accompanied the grand undertakings of the State Hospital. The majestic pipe organ, once a source of pride and aspiration, has vanished without a trace. The Congregate Dining Hall, reduced to rubble, is now pressed beneath the asphalt. The radio broadcasts that once carried messages of hope across the airwaves have left no recordings behind to capture their fleeting promise. And Everlasting Life, Dr. Harrington's unfinished opus, endures only in its text, while its music is lost to time, its notes unheard and its melodies left to the imagination.

Yet Howard remains; transformed nearly beyond recognition, but still here. The landscape may have shifted, and the buildings replaced, but one cannot help but feel something intangible persists— the ghost of a memory that refuses to fade, lingering like the familiar refrain of a song long forgotten, and as enduring as the land itself.

Alone, I turned to trace my steps back along Howard Avenue, over cracked and weedy sidewalks, and made my way home.

ORGAN SPECIFICATIONS

There are over 1,300 pipes in this organ, these with augmenting super and sub couplers produce the effect of over 3,000 pipes. The cable from the console to the organ contains about 600 wires which are finally distributed to the various chests and controls of the organ proper. There is a kinetic blower and generator of ample capacity, the latter agitating the magnets of the organ. The blower, motor, and generator are in the basement of the building, enclosed in a chamber especially constructed for the purpose. The air to blower is taken from a room on the Congregate Dining Hall floor, having the same temperature as the Hall, which is always warm.

The console is placed in front and to the left, a distance of 20' from the organ, permitting the player at all times to have a full view of the director, the choir and also of the entire audience. The player at that distance is able to hear the same effects of the organ as do others.

GREAT ORGAN

Open Diapason	8'	61 Pipes
Dopple Flute	8'	61 Pipes
Gamba	8'	61 Pipes
Gamba Celeste	8'	61 Pipes
Tuba (Enlarged Trumpet Reed)	8'	61 Pipes
Harmonic Flute	4'	61 Pipes

GREAT COUPLERS

Great to Great Super	4'
Swell to Great	4'
Swell to Great	8'
Swell to Great	16'
Choir to Great	8'
Choir to Great	16'

Three Composition Pistons to affect Great and Pedal Stops.

SWELL ORGAN

Bourdon	16'	61 Pipes
Open Diapason	8'	61 Pipes
Stop Flute	8'	61 Pipes
Viol d'Orchestra	8'	61 Pipes
Vox Celeste	8'	61 Pipes
Wald Flute	4'	61 Pipes
Flautino	2'	61 Pipes
Horn Oboe	8'	61 Pipes
Vox Humana (Set off in Separate Swell Box)	8'	61 Pipes
Chimes		20 Notes

Termolo (Affecting all three manuals)

SWELL COUPLERS

Swell to Swell Super	4'
Swell to Swell Sub	4'

Three Composition Pistons to affect Swell and Pedal Stops.

CHOIR ORGAN

Violin Diapason	8'	61 Pipes
Dulciana	8'	61 Pipes
Melodia	8'	61 Pipes
Flute D'Amour	4'	61 Pipes
Piccolo	2'	61 Pipes
Clarinet	8'	61 Pipes
Chimes		20 Notes
Harp		56 Notes
Xylophone		48 Notes

CHOIR COUPLERS

Choir to Choir Super	4'
Choir to Choir Sub	16'
Swell to Choir	8'

Two Composition Pistons to affect Choir and Pedal Organ

PEDAL ORGAN

Violinello	8'	61 Pipes
Bourdon	16'	61 Pipes
Open Diapason	16'	61 Pipes

PEDAL COUPLERS

Swell to Pedal	4'
Great to Pedal	16'
Choir to Pedal	8'

PEDAL MOVEMENTS

Balanced Swell Pedal
Balanced Choir Pedal
Grand Crescendo Pedal controlling all
stops from the softest to full organ.

Dedication Day Program
May 16, 1926

March of the Priests from Athalie	Mr. Truesdale
Song of the World's Adventurers – Converse	Festival Chorus
Londonderry Air – Coleman	Mr. Truesdale
Save Me O God – Randegger	Lucy Marsh Gordon
Let Their Celestial Concerts All Unite from Sampson – Handel	Festival Chorus
Melodie – Huerter	Mr. Truesdale
Grand March from Aida – Verdi	Festival Chorus
Introduction in E-flat – Jacobs	Mr. Bolan
Procedenti ab Utroque from Tantum Ergo – arr. by Novella	Mr. Bolan
There's a Beautiful Land on High – Mrs. Taylor	Lucy Marsh Gordon
Dance of the Bacchantes – Gounod	Festival Chorus
Lovely Night – Offenbach	Festival Chorus
Solveig's Lied – Grieg	Mr. Truesdale
Hallelujah – Handel	Festival Chorus

To experience the music of the Dedication Day Program, scan the QR code below to access a curated playlist.

About Everlasting Life

Everlasting Life was Dr. Arthur Harrington's final creative work—a poem published posthumously by his children, originally conceived with musical scores that are now lost; only the text remains. Written in his later years, this ambitious piece uses mythological figures to explore the themes that defined his life's work—the power of transformation and humanity's journey toward progress. Presented here in full, it stands as both a meditation on the present and a hopeful vision for the future, where the human spirit, guided by enlightenment, can achieve lasting peace.

EVERLASTING LIFE

BY

ARTHUR H. HARRINGTON, M.D.

A PHANTASY

SYMBOLIZING
THE MATERIAL AND SPIRITUAL EVOLUTION
OF GENUS HOMO

PART ONE

YMIR SPEAKS

The Frost-King Boasts His Power

He Proclaims His Fell Purpose

INTERLUDE

Twentieth-Century Glimpses of Our Earth and Man

PART TWO

HELIOS SPEAKS

*The Benign Giver of Life Prepares Our Planet
for Man's Habitation*

He Presages the Soul's Goal

INTERPRETATION

THESE POEMS, while phantasy, are presented as symbolic of world truths, material and spiritual, of past, present and future ages. Ymir (the Frost-King in mythological lore) and Helios (the Sun-God of the ancients) are designed to symbolize the age-old struggles, Ymir representing states ever placing obstacles in the path of human progress. Ymir stands for ignorance, superstition, greed, injustice, tragedies brought by man upon brother man. Ymir would end all advance, material and spiritual. Helios, the mind of man always in the making, would raise him to the "nth" power of his benign potentialities. Helios stands for energies acting through all time, directing the Mind and Soul of man toward the goal of UNIVERSAL BROTHERHOOD AND WORLD ENDURING PEACE.

PART ONE

YMIR
SPEAKS

List to me! The mighty Frost-King.
No idle boast my voice shall ring,
But truth I here in full reveal,
My deeds entire I will unseal;
My purpose too shall be made plain;
Know well! There's reason in my reign.
To rule this earth my fixed goal;
To spread my realm from Pole to Pole;
That's solely means to one great end;—
To destroy life—You hear?—attend!

Imperial scepter here behold
Is symbol of my power untold.
No human king has ever known
A semblance of the might I own.
Enough! Judge what the future holds.
This earth perforce my past unfolds.
Men of science read the signs well;
Glacial Age tells you what befell.

From high mount of Arctic Ice-Cap
There opened out the World-Wide Map;
Far to the South and distant East,
Your lands and isles, the very least,
Your towering mountain slopes, I saw
Must all be subject to my Law;
Hills, valleys, vasty plains, as well
As inland seas; I could foretell
Of all the Eastern World the fate
Which on my lone decree did wait.

To Western World I turned my glance;
There Glacial Epoch made advance.

To your great plains and Rocky's slope,
None of your lands was too remote;
My glaciers their deep channels wrought;
To your great rivers bars were brought;
Your inland seas were plains of ice
Held by ever-tightening vice.
All this the hand of Ymir wrought,
Wher'er I walked there Life was naught.

Enough! The means I have portrayed;
My purpose only is delayed:
All Life on Earth is here condemned;
My aim and end without amend.
I sealed this globe with ice-garb dense;
Ages none came to your defense
Till distant Helios scanning space
Turned to your Planet His full face.

I knew His subtle purpose well,
To sire a Realm where Life would dwell.
Through constant circuit He has rode,
But cannot pierce to mine abode.
This is a Titan struggle know.
He'll find in me eternal foe.

I've slumbered, but My Spirit wakes,
My rampant Soul fresh armor takes.
Know well I shall advance again.
Proud Helios will strive in vain.
From Pole to Pole I'll seal this Globe;
No wave of warmth shall pierce its robe.
For aye this mundane sphere I'll lock
In walls as adamant as rock.

INTERLUDE

Erebus veiled in night the Earth,
Resplendent stars their stations took,
Faded on air the sounds of mirth,
The toilers of the day sought rest;
Murmuring Lethe courted sleep,
Tired eyelids heeded her request.

In time came faintest hint of dawn,
Each measured moment changes wrought,
Night's sable robes were straight withdrawn,
Red crest proclaimed his clarion call,
From forest songsters matins poured,
Life to another day woke all.

Like fingers of an unseen palm
From eastern sky shot shafts of light,
Tasks for skilled painters to embalm.
Helios His golded brow disclosed;
Soon came his smiling full-orbed face;
His rays the wide terrain surveyed.

He viewed great mountains, lesser hills,
Forests noble and rolling plains,
Glistening rivers and laughing rills;
Calm lakes His mirrored face retained.
All nature smiled and laughed in turn,
Awaking Life her source proclaimed.

Aside from Nature's pageantry
Came every phase of human life
Disclosing to His Majesty
The precious winnings man has made,
The triumphs of his brawn and brain
The problems solved, by science weighed.

Swiftly came other scenes in view,
Multitudes, life's bare needs denied,
Frustrate, their burdened days renew:
The enginery of modern war,
Using forces man has tamed
To scorn the weight of Moral Law

Razing great and glorious cities,
Crushing the lives of innocents,
Mindless of inhumanities,
Ruthlessly heedless of the loss;
But:—Do not for the Soul despair,
Hear now the words of Helios.

PART TWO

HELIOS
SPEAKS

Before the race of man was born,
Before the human concept Time,
As well before man's sense of Space,
There was, as now, Eternity.
For eons on unknown eons
With bewildering speed propelled
A nebulous mass rolled on,
A whorl of clouds and vapor.
I, Helios, in the center rode,
Acme of incandescence,
Cosmic source of Light and Life.

The question you may fairly ask,
Where bound this speed-compelling mass?
Were You an aimless wanderer
In this infinite void of voids?
Nay! For unmeasured time on time
My vast potentials well I knew,
Aware that in this flaming flux
Were held the stuffs which planets make.
Ancient Peoples called me Sun-God.

While in mystic tongue they spoke,
These myths were symbolized truths.
In Helios alone resides,
From Helios alone proceeds
Cataclysmic, transilient might.

But mind you these surpassing powers
In action howsomever wrought,
In crashing, paroxysmal throes,
Or pouring ambient rays abroad,
Through all there ran a purpose fixed,
To stage a LIFE-ABOUNDING world;
That, my eternal will and aim.
Seen you now the distant heavens;
Behold there in perfect balance,
Pursuing their allotted paths
Those bodies with your chosen names,
Mercury, Venus, Saturn, Mars,
Jupiter, Uranus, Neptune.
There's still another you call Earth.
These planets and your Earth as well
Were once a part of my vast sphere.
I hurled them into waiting space
Where through the ages they have sped
Obedient to my behest.

For Earth I mapped a special path;
I planned a highway so defined,
So distanced in its complete course,
So spaced its days, its nights, its tides,
From surface to its inner depths

X

Plethoric with material stores,
Responsive to My energies,
Making thus an alembic vast,
A furnished laboratory,
Where all My laws would be released,

Where EVERLASTING LIFE would stream;
That, for your Earth alone, my aim.

Before your planet could serve life
A fit abode must be ordained
'Twas first a molten world of stuffs,
A massive and ebullient flux.
Go read your story in the rocks;
Find interplay of force and rhythm.
In grotesque shapes they will be found,
Some are tilted, some are bent,
Sedimentary masses rent,
Era superposed on era.
Then came the long Azoic Age;
Tides spreading and receding
Over shoals of mud and sand,
In time transformed to slates and shales.
Such records and others you'll find.

Then dawned the Protozoan Age.
As untold eons counted gains,
Amoeba, pristine spark of Life,
Ope'd new paths for energies;
These through many strange diversions,
By countless sublimations wrought,

Led to a self-conscious being—
By that token GENUS HOMO—
Harbinger of intelligence,
Destined by attributes thus gained,
Through hierarchy of the MIND
To reach nearer, and nearer still,
The goal of EVERLASTING LIFE

Birth-throes of your material world
Long preceded fairest regions.
Such changes are but prototypes
Of pains the human race must bear
On its reach to loftier plains.

Hear now the last words of Helios
Why invoke EVERLASTING LIFE?
Record this answer for all time:—

To draw lessons from the Ages,
To banish all destructive force
Retarding to man's destiny.
There'll come Leaders, and more Leaders,
Teachers of Hygiene of the Soul—
My purpose alway before them
To raise man to his highest plain—
This the will and aim of Helios
To give this being with a Soul
The path to his supernal right,
A UNIVERSAL BROTHERHOOD,
A WORLD OF LASTING PEACE.

BIBLIOGRAPHY

THE DEATH OF GEORGE F. KEENE, SUPERINTENDENT OF THE STATE HOSPITAL FOR THE INSANE

"Dr. Keene Seriously Ill." *The Providence Journal*, March 10, 1905, p. 5.

"Dr. Keene's Condition Serious." *The Providence Journal*, March 11, 1905, p. 4.

"George F. Keene, Noted Alienist: Superintendent of the State Hospital for the Insane Died Yesterday." *The Providence Journal*, March 14, 1905, p. 4.

"Many Attend Funeral Service: Obsequies of Dr. George F. Keene Held at Howard Yesterday Afternoon." *The Providence Journal*, March 17, 1905, p. 2.

THE CONGREGATE DINING HALL AT THE STATE HOSPITAL FOR THE INSANE, HOWARD, RHODE ISLAND

"New Buildings: Plans for Improvements at State Insane Hospital." *The Providence Journal*, March 9, 1899, p. 9.

"General Assembly: House Passed Appropriations for New Buildings for Insane." *The Providence Journal*, April 4, 1900, p. 12.

"Visited Danvers: Securing Ideas for New Dining Hall at Howard." *The Providence Journal*, January 26, 1903, p. 3.

"State's Largest Dining Hall." *The Providence Journal*, August 1, 1903.

"At the State Hospital for the Insane." *The Providence Journal*, October 25, 1903, p. 20.

"Great Improvements at the Rhode Island State Hospital for the Insane." *The Providence Journal*, October 25, 1903, p. 20.

RENAMING THE STATE HOSPITAL FOR THE INSANE

"Treatment of Insane: Suggestion That the Asylum Be Separated from the State Farm." *The Providence Journal*, September 17, 1894, p. 6.

"The State Insane: Proposed Bill to Amend Certain Conditions at Howard." *The Providence Journal*, May 17, 1897, p. 10.

"State Hospital for Insane: Dr. George W. Keene Now Superintendent Under the New Law [sic]." *The Providence Journal*, June 23, 1897, p. 10.

WILLIAM MORSE AND RELATED EVENTS

"Adjudged Insane: Motorman William Morse Reported As Missing, Reappeared Yesterday." *The Providence Journal*, October 23, 1902, p. 12.

"Morse Violent: Fought with Insane Fury When Arraigned in District Court." *The Providence Journal*, March 17, 1903, pp. 1–3.

"Will Be Kept at the Jail." *The Providence Journal*, March 18, 1903, p. 12.

"Many Mourners: Funeral of Miss Toombs, Victim of Sunday's Murder." *The Providence Journal*, March 19, 1903, p. 12.

"Had No Orders But Arrested Morse on His Own Responsibility." *The Providence Journal*, March 27, 1903, p. 9.

"Atkins's Story: Man Whom Miss Toombs Appealed Testified." *The Providence Journal*, March 31, 1903, p. 13.

"Navy's Answer: Denies Responsibility in Morse Case." *The Providence Journal*, June 6, 1903, p. 12.

"For Murder: True Bill Against William Stevens Morse." *The Providence Journal*, June 16, 1903, p. 12.

"Board of Charities Dismisses Dr. Jewett." *The Providence Journal*, January 16, 1907, p. 1.

SARAT MUKERJI AND STATE INVESTIGATIONS

"Novice Employed At State Hospital." *The Providence Journal*, April 13, 1928, p. 4.

"Dr. Johnson Ousted From State Hospital." *The Providence Journal*, April 14, 1928, pp. 1-4.

"State Hospital Head Dismisses Sarat C. Mukerji." *The Providence Journal*, July 11, 1928, p. 1.

"State House Brevities." *The Providence Journal*, July 13, 1928, p. 22.

"Investigators Would Abolish Present State Welfare Board and Director." *The Providence Journal*, December 23, 1928, p. 6.

"Report Condemns Facilities At Women's Reformatory." *The Providence Journal*, December 24, 1928, p. 13.

"Report Condemns School Facilities." *The Providence Journal*, December 24, 1928, p. 16.

"'Filthy' Jail Approved By Welfare Commission." *The Providence Journal*, December 25, 1928, p. 15.

"Bad Conditions Revealed at State Home and School." *The Providence Journal*, December 27, 1928, p. 13.

"Report Criticizes Overturn In State Hospital Staff." *The Providence Journal*, December 28, 1928, pp. 13-15.

"Investigators Find Morale At State Hospital Broken." *The Providence Journal*, December 29, 1928, p. 13.

"Change Urged in Make-Up of Public Welfare Board." *The Providence Journal*, January 2, 1929, p. 13.

"Welfare Board of Three Instead of Nine Advocated." *The Providence Journal*, January 3, 1929, p. 13.

DR. RANSOM SARTWELL

"Frank Weeden, Escaped Maniac, Admits Killing Dr. Sartwell; Caught In Warwick at 3 A.M." *The Providence Journal*, January 13, 1929, pp. 1–2.

"Weeden Safely Shut Up for Life." *The Providence Journal*, January 27, 1929, p. 3.

"Hospital Head Slayer a Suicide in His Cell." *The New York Times*, December 24, 1929, p. 10.

"Criminal Insane Ward Will Open Before March 1." *The Providence Journal*, January 3, 1931, pp. 1, 5.

STATE REPORTS AND FINDINGS

Board of State Charities and Corrections. *Annual Reports of the Board of State Charities and Corrections of Rhode Island, Volumes 11–13* (1879–1881). Providence: State of Rhode Island.

Board of State Charities and Corrections. *Thirty-Second Annual Report of the Board of State Charities and Corrections.* Providence: State of Rhode Island, 1900.

Board of State Charities and Corrections. *Annual Reports of the Board of State Charities and Corrections of Rhode Island, Volumes 33–37* (1901–1905). Providence: State of Rhode Island.

"State Hospital Needs Described." *The Providence Journal*, January 15, 1926, p. 26.

State Public Welfare Commission. *Annual Reports, 1926/27–1928/29.* Providence: State of Rhode Island.

Arthur H. Harrington and Contributions

Harrington, Arthur H., M.D. "The Congregate Dining-Room and Its Management." *American Journal of Psychiatry*, Volume 70, Number 2 (1913): p. 127 et seq.

Harrington, Arthur H., M.D. *The Story of the State Hospital Pipe Organ.* Providence, R.I.: E.L. Freeman, 1926.

"Weeden Is Caught; Can Escape Again." *The Providence Journal*, April 21, 1926, p. 1.

"Dr. Harrington, State Hospital Director, Quits." *The Providence Journal*, July 18, 1926, pp. 1–2.

"Dr. Harrington Will Aid State Hospital." *The Providence Journal*, August 14, 1926, p. 20.

"Friends Honor Dr. Harrington." *The Providence Journal*, October 2, 1926, p. 1.

Harrington, Arthur H. "Music as a Therapeutic Aid in a Hospital for Mental Diseases." Paper presented in Paris, France, 1930. Translated into French and published in *Archives Internationales de Neurologie.* Later published in *Mental Hygiene*, Volume 23, 1939.

"Dr. Harrington Stricken Fatally." *The Providence Journal*, March 13, 1939, pp. 5–6.

Munro, Walter Lee, M.D. "An Appreciation." Editorial. *Rhode Island Medical Journal*, Volume 21–22 (June 1939): 105.

The State Hospital Pipe Organ and Radio Broadcasts

"Blind Pianist Will Accompany Choir." *The Providence Journal*, October 9, 1925, p. 24.

"Concert Broadcast By Hospital Choir." *The Providence Journal*, October 10, 1925, p. 18.

"State Asylum Can Get $7500 Organ." *The Providence Journal,* November 6, 1925, p. 2.

"History of Organ Fund Is Broadcast." *The Providence Journal,* December 3, 1925, p. 15.

"Concert Planned at State Hospital." *The Providence Journal,* May 13, 1926, p. 13.

"Organ Is Dedicated At State Hospital." *The Providence Journal,* May 17, 1926, p. 4.

HISTORICAL OVERVIEWS

Jones, Henry A., M.D. *The Dark Days of Social Welfare at the State Institutions at Howard, Rhode Island.* 1943.

DeSilva, Bruce. "Are We Not Our Brothers Keeper?" *The Providence Sunday Journal,* December 6, 1981, p. 5 et seq.

Golden, Janet, and Eric C. Schneider. "Custody and Control: The Rhode Island State Hospital for Mental Diseases, 1870-1970." *Rhode Island History* 41, no. 4 (November 1982): 113-125.

EVERLASTING LIFE

Harrington, Arthur H., M.D. *Everlasting Life: A Phantasy Symbolizing the Material and Spiritual Evolution of Genus Homo.* Privately printed. Boston, 1939.

PHOTOGRAPHIC REFERENCES

Cover (Front): *The pipe organ on the musician's balcony of the Congregate Dining Hall, State Hospital for Mental Diseases, 1926.* From: Harrington, Arthur H., M.D. *The Story of the State Hospital Pipe Organ.* Providence, R.I.: E.L. Freeman, 1926.

Cover (Back): *The Service Building, which served as an entrance to the Congregate Dining Hall, State Hospital for Mental Diseases, circa 1905-1912.* From the author's collection.

Frontispiece: Dr. Arthur H. Harrington. Original photograph courtesy of John Gray; signature digitally added by the author.

Page 2: *The Congregate Dining Hall at the State Hospital for Mental Diseases, circa 1926.* From: Harrington, Arthur H., M.D. *The Story of the State Hospital Pipe Organ.* Providence, R.I.: E.L. Freeman, 1926.

Page 7: *The Chapel Choir of the State Hospital for the Insane, circa 1900–1912.* From the author's personal collection.

Page 9: *Floral Arrangements at Dr. Keene's Funeral, March 17, 1905.* From: *The Providence Journal,* March 17, 1905, p. 2.

Page 15: *The playing of tubular chimes is the signal for each of the several steps in the serving of a meal in the congregate dining hall.* From the author's collection.

Page 16: *The Congregate Dining Hall at the State Hospital for Mental Diseases, circa 1900–1912, before the installation of the pipe organ.* From the author's collection.

Page 26: *The pipe organ and choir at the Congregate Dining Hall, State Hospital for Mental Diseases, 1926.* From: Harrington, Arthur H., M.D. *The Story of the State Hospital Pipe Organ.* Providence, R.I.: E.L. Freeman, 1926.

Page 36: *Howard Avenue in Cranston, Rhode Island, 2024.* Photograph by the author.